故园画忆

庚寅中秋 韩磐达 题

《故园画忆系列》编委会

名誉主任：韩启德

主　　任：邵　鸿

委　　员：（按姓氏笔画为序）

万　捷	王秋桂	方李莉	叶培贵
刘魁立	严绍璗	吴为山	况　晗
邵　鸿	范　芳	范贻光	岳庆平
郑培凯	孟　白	唐晓峰	曹兵武

故园画忆系列
Memory of the Old Home in Sketches

上海滩上的万国风情

International Styles of Old Shanghai

底谓 绘画撰文
Sketches & Notes by Di Wei

学苑出版社
Academy Press

图书在版编目（CIP）数据

上海滩上的万国风情/底谓绘画、撰文. —— 北京：学苑出版社，2015.5
（故园画忆系列）（2021.6重印）
ISBN 978-7-5077-4773-7

Ⅰ.①上… Ⅱ.①底… Ⅲ.①钢笔画—作品集—中国—现代 ②上海市—概况 Ⅳ.①J224 ②K925.1

中国版本图书馆CIP数据核字(2015)第100851号

出 版 人：	孟　白
责任编辑：	杨　雷
出版发行：	学苑出版社
社　　址：	北京市丰台区南方庄2号院1号楼
邮政编码：	100079
网　　址：	www.book001.com
电子信箱：	xueyuanpress@163.com
联系电话：	010-67601101（营销部）、010-67603091（总编室）
印 刷 厂：	河北赛文印刷有限公司
开本尺寸：	889×1194 1/24
印　　张：	7.75
字　　数：	15千字
图　　幅：	162幅
版　　次：	2015年11月北京第1版
印　　次：	2021年6月北京第2次印刷
定　　价：	60.00元

目 录

自　序　　　　　　　　　　　　　底谓

安仁街、北京东路、广东路等

九曲桥	3
格林邮船大楼	4
国华商业银行大楼	5
益丰洋行	6
四明银行大楼	7
雷士德医学院	8
百老汇大厦	9
上海邮政总局	10
大上海博物馆	11
提篮桥监狱	12
徐家汇藏书楼	13
震旦大学博物馆	14
大千胜境石牌坊	15
南洋兄弟烟草公司	16
耶松船厂	17
雷士德工学院	18
仁记洋行	19
业广地产有限公司	20
比利时领事馆	21
海关俱乐部	22
美国花旗总会	23
妇产科医院	24
同济德文医学工学堂图书馆	25
日清轮船公司	26
永年人寿保险公司	27
三菱洋行	28
中央造币厂	29
江南造船厂	30
江湾体育场	31
美国学校	32
中国福利会儿童艺术剧院	33
南洋公学图书馆	34
中法学堂	35
恩派亚大戏院	36
国泰大戏院	37
法租界巡捕房	38
法租界公董局	39
礼查饭店	40
俄罗斯领事馆	41
上海储能中学一分部	42
虹口大旅社	43
浙江第一商业银行	44
公共租界工部局	45
《申报》报馆	46
美童公学	47
亚洲文会北中国支会	48
光陆大戏院	49
商船会馆	50
徐汇公学崇思楼	51

九江路、浦东南路、四川路等

原德华银行旧址	55
沪江大学图书馆	56
美琪大戏院	57
中西女塾	58
礼和洋行大楼	59
汉弥尔登大楼	60
建设大厦	61
清心女中	62
英侨业余戏剧协会剧场	63
永安公司大楼	64
汇中饭店	65
上海电力公司大楼	66
先施公司	67
慈昌大厦	68
新新公司	69
大新公司	70
新世界游乐场	71
华安人寿保险公司	72
四行储蓄会大楼	73
大光明电影院	74
跑马总会	75
犹太人总会	76
同孚大楼	77
法童学堂	78
法国总会	79
英美颐中烟草股份有限公司	80
上海特别市政府	81
上海天文台	82
上海证券交易所	83
上海市政府（民国）	84
广慈医院	85
沪宁铁路总公司大楼	86
商务印书馆	87
中国银行虹口大楼	88
企业大楼	89
美孚洋行大楼	90
卜内门洋碱有限公司办公楼	91
三井物产公司上海支店	92
汇丰大楼	93
四行储蓄大楼	94
东亚银行大楼	95
里白渡桥	96
外白渡桥	97
三山会馆	98
新亚大酒楼	99
沪宁铁路上海站(北站)大楼	100
西区污水处理厂泵房	101
三角地菜场	102
圣约翰大学办公楼	103
圣约翰大学思颜堂	104
圣约翰大学韬奋楼	105
圣约翰大学体育室	106
圣约翰大学西门堂	107
圣约翰大学格致室	108
民立中学办公楼	109
中国红十字会医院	110
虹口救火会	111
大上海大戏院	112
大世界游乐场	113

东方饭店	114
上海银行同业公会	115

延安东路、延安西路、中山东路等

中汇大厦	119
华商纱布交易所	120
洋泾浜气象信号台	121
德士古大楼	122
南京大戏院	123
宏恩医院	124
意大利总会	125
美国乡村总会	126
安倍洋行办公楼	127
上海自然科学研究所	128
第四中山大学医学院	129
杨树浦发电厂	130
杨树浦水厂	131
怡和纱厂	132
百乐门舞厅	133
海底电缆登陆局房	134
乍浦路桥	135
中国通商银行	136
亚细亚火油公司大楼	137
英国总会	138
有利银行	139
大北电报公司	140
上海轮船招商局	141
汇丰银行	142
华俄道胜银行	143
上海海关大楼	144
交通银行	145
台湾银行	146
《字林西报》报馆	147
麦加利银行	148
中国银行大楼	149
沙逊大厦	150
正金银行	151
扬子大楼	152
东方汇理银行上海分行	153
怡和洋行办公楼	154
英国总领事馆	155
十六铺码头	156
上海电话局南市总局	157

其他

白鹤塘湾桥	161
放生桥	162
望仙桥	163
济渡桥	164
古漪园	165
学宫牌坊	166
州桥	167
报童	168
修伞匠	169
弹花匠	170
剃头匠	171
沪上印度人	172
修铜匠	173

Contents

Preface   Di Wei

Anren Street, East Beijing Road, Guangdong Road, etc.

Nine Zigzag Bridge	3
Glen Line Building	4
Former China State Bank Building	5
Former Abraham E Building	6
Former Building of Siming Bank	7
Former Henry Lester Institute of Medical Research	8
Former Broadway Mansion	9
Former General Post Office	10
Former Shanghai Museum	11
Tilanqiao Prison	12
Bibliotheca Zikawei	13
Museum of Aurora University	14
Archway Gate with Numerous Stones	15
Former Nanyang Brothers Tobacco	16
Former Shipyard of S.C.	17
Former Lester School and Henry Lester Institute of Technical Education	18
Former Gibb, Livingston & Co.	19
Former Landwide Estates Co., Ltd Building	20
Former Consulate General of the Kingdom of Belgium	21
Former Customs Club of China	22
The Former American Club	23
Former Obstetrics & Gynecology Hospital	24
Former Deutsche Ingenieurschule Library	25
Former Japan-China Steamship Company	26
Former Yongnian Life Insurance Company	27
Former Mitsubishi Company	28
Former Central Mint	29
Former Jiangnan Shipyard	30
Former Jiangwan Stadium	31
Former American School	32
Children's Theatre of China Welfare Institute (CWI)	33
Former Nan Yang Public School Library	34
Former Sino-French School	35
Empire Theater	36
Former Cathay Theatre	37
Former Municipal Police, French Concession	38
Former Conseil D'Administration Municipale de la Concession Française de Shanghai	39
Former British Richard Astor House	40
Consulate General of Russia	41
A Part of the Former Shanghai Chunneng Middle School	42
Former Hongkou Hotel	43
Former Chekiang Commercial Bank	44
Former Municipal Council of the Shanghai International Settlement	45
Former Building of the *Shanghai News*	46
Former Shanghai American School	47
Former Site of the North China Branch of the Royal Asiatic Society	48
Former Capitol Theatre	49
Former Merchant Shipping Guildhall	50
Former Chongsi Building of the Xuhui Public School	51

Jiujiang Road, South Pudong Road, Sichuan Road, etc.

Former Site of Deutsche Asiatische Bank	55
Former Library of Shanghai University	56
The Majestic Theatre	57
Former McTyeire School	58
Former Building of Carlowitz & Co.	59
Former Hamilton House	60
The Construction Building	61
Former Mary Farnham Girls' School	62
Former British-Chinese Amateur Drama Club	63
Former Wing On Department Store	64
Former Palace Hotel	65
Former Building of Shanghai Power Company	66
The Former Sincere Company	67
Former Cichang Building	68
The Former Sun Sun Company	69
Former Sun Co., Ltd	70
Former New World Amusement Arcade	71
Former Building of Hua'an Life Insurance Company	72
Former Building for the Savings Society of Four Banks	73
Shanghai Ever-Shining Circuit Cinema	74
Former Race Club	75
Former Jewish Club	76
Yates Apartments	77
Former Shanghai French School	78
Former College Francais	79
Former British-American YeeTsoong Tobacco Co.,Ltd	80
Former Special Municipal Government of Shanghai	81
Shanghai Astronomical Observatory	82
Shanghai Stock Exchange	83
Fomer Municipal Government of Shanghai	84
Former St. Marie Hospital	85
Former Office Building of the Shanghai and Nanjing Railway Company	86
Former Commercial Press Building	87
Former Hongkou Branch of the Bank of China	88
Former Enterprise Building	89
Former Standard-Vacuum Oil Building	90
Former Office Building of the British Brunner, Mond & Co., Ltd	91
Former Mitsui Bussan Kaisha Co.,Ltd, Shanghai Branch	92
New Building of the Hong Kong and Shanghai Banking Corporation (HSBC)	93
Former Building for the Saving Society of Four Banks on Hankou Road	94
Former Building of the Shanghai Branch of the Bank of East Asia	95
Libaidu Bridge	96
Waibaidu Bridge	97
Sanshan Guildhall	98
The Former Shanghai New Asia Hotel	99
Former Shanghai Station (Shanghai North Station) of the Shanghai-Nanjing Railway	100
The Former Pump House of the West District Sewage Treatment Plant	101
Former Delta Grocery Market	102
Office Building of Saint John's University	103
Siyan Hall of Saint John's University	104
Taofen Building of Saint John's University	105
Stadium of Saint John's University	106
Ximen Hall of Saint John's University	107
Gezhi Chamber of Saint John's University	108
Former Office Building of Minli High School	109
Former China Red Cross Hospital	110
Former Hongkew Fire Station	111

Former Metropol Theatre	112
Former Great World Amusement Park	113
The Former Dong Fang Hotel	114
Former Shanghai Banking Association	115

Yan'an Road, West Yan'an Road, East Zhongshan Road, etc.

Former Building of the New Chung Wei Bank	119
Former Shanghai Cotton Goods Exchange	120
Former Gutzlaff Signal Tower	121
Former Texaco Building	122
Former Nanjing Grand Theatre	123
Former Hong'en Hospital	124
Former Italian Club	125
Former Columbia Country Club	126
Former Office Building of Swiss Ampire Company	127
Former Shanghai Institute of Natural Science	128
Medical College of the Fourth Zhongshan University	129
Yangshupu Power Plant	130
Yangshupu Water Plant	131
Former Jardine Cotton Mill	132
Former Paramount Ballroom	133
Former Building of the Office for Joining Land and Submarine Cables	134
Zhapu Road Bridge	135
Former Commercial Bank of China	136
The Former British and Royal Dutch Shell's Asiatic Petroleum Division	137
Former British Club	138
Former Building of Mercantile Bank of India, London, and China	139
Former Great Northern Telegraph Corporation	140
China Merchants Steamship Navigation Company	141
Former HSBC Building	142
Former Building of the Russo-Chinese Bank	143
Shanghai Customs House	144
Former Building of China Bank of Communications	145
Former Building of the Japanese Bank of Taiwan	146
Building of Former *North China Daily News*	147
Former Chartered Bank of India, Australia, and China	148
Bank of China Building	149
The Former Sassoon House	150
Former Yokohama Specie Bank	151
Yangtze Insurance Building	152
Former Shanghai Branch of the French Banque de l'Indochine	153
Former British Jardine Matheson Building	154
The Former Consulate General of the United Kingdom	155
16-Shop Wharf	156
Former Nanshi Branch of Shanghai Telephone Office	157

Others

Tangwan Bridge	161
Fangsheng Bridge	162
Wangxian Bridge	163
Jidu Bridge	164
Guyi Garden	165
Memorial Archway Gates, Chongming Academy	166
Zhouqiao Bridge	167
Paperboy	168
Umbrella Repairer	169
Cotton-Fluffing Bedding	170
Barber	171
Indians in Shanghai	172
Coppersmith	173

自 序

一方面，世人对上海这座东方大都市多另眼相看，因为它似乎有着明显的西方"血缘"；另一方面，世人又对西方的"文艺复兴"和"启蒙运动"肃然起敬，因为这两场运动对于西方的现代化，具有决定性的意义。然而，若要读懂上海这座城市，就不得不将其命运与西方的"文艺复兴"和"启蒙运动"联系起来，因为它们实属一脉相承！

欧洲14世纪中叶至17世纪初发生了一场波澜壮阔的思想文化革命——文艺复兴运动。其源起于佛罗伦萨、米兰和威尼斯，最终遍及全欧。该运动的核心是：提出以人为中心而非以神为中心，肯定人的价值和尊严。也正因为文艺复兴运动倡导对人类自身价值的尊重，科学在人类的生存中第一次得到了高度重视。而科学所揭示出的诸多奥秘，不仅撼动了宗教的神权威严，导致规模工业的出现，影响了人们的生活，推动了文化艺术的进步，而且还促使以资本为基础之资产阶级的形成。

由于科技的支持，西方诸国（尤其是英、法等国）在工业、军事、航海等多领域迅速强大起来。它们强势要求仍处于封建体制的中国政府，开放国门，进行自由贸易。这两种政治体制的矛盾，很快于1840年，以鸦片为导火索上升为战争。结果，代表当时先进科学技术和政治制度的资产阶级，在这场战争中取得了胜利。于是，它们挑挑拣拣，将既有江海航运之利，又居南北之中的上海，圈作新的通商口岸。1843年上海开埠。

启蒙运动的烈火从此烧到了上海！

资产阶级进入上海后，并非仅仅是做些买卖而已，而是将资产阶级所取得的所有成就，全方位地灌输进来。在中国这个以农业为本的国度里，开辟了一块资产阶级能够随心所欲的领地。他们以"自由贸易"为由，开设起了银行、证券、保险、远洋运输、石油等各种实业；并以"租借地"为根据地，开设了自来水、电灯、电话、电报、医疗乃至铁路等公共事业；甚至还开设了博彩、舞厅、剧院、电影院等娱乐业。

更重要的是，资产阶级将上海打造成了一块"目无王法"的自由世界。他们设立教堂，传播契约文化，宣扬三权分立的政治制度；兴办圣约翰大学等中、高级教育机构，传授科学技术知识，从而在政治上动摇了中国封建皇权的尊严。以至于很快在中国封建统治阶级内部，开始出现了政治思想的分化。1861年具有民族资产阶级色彩的洋务运动，以"自强"为旗号，学习并采纳西方的先进技术，创办中国现代军工业，如在上海开办了江南制造局。

好了，当我们了解了上述这些文脉之后，再打开这本书，走进上海这座突然崛起于20世纪前半叶的东方大都市，便不难理解，那些建筑是因何而生的了。

是为序。

底　谓
2014年初夏于黄浦之滨

Preface

People often think Shanghai, an oriental "cosmopolis", is different from other Chinese cities, because it apparently displays elements of Western origins. With the critical importance of the modernization of the Western world, the Renaissance Period and the Enlightenment Movement are universally respected; therefore, to fully understand Shanghai, it is necessary to connect its past with those movements, for they share the same roots.

From the mid-14th to the early 17th century, the Renaissance, as a revolution of culture and thought, swept Europe. Starting from Florence, Milan and Venice, it eventually spread to the rest of Europe. It focused on the human rather than God by fully recognizing human value and dignity. It is exactly because of its advocacy of respect for human value that science was, for the first time, highly valued in history. By revealing many mysteries, science challenged God's supremacy, led to the industry of scale, influenced people's lives, advanced culture and art, and gave birth to the bourgeoisie with the accumulation of capital.

On the back of scientific advancement, Western states, especially the United Kingdom and France, developed rapidly in such areas as industry, military and navigation. So they forced China to open the door to free trade, when the country was ruled by a feudal government. Conflicts between the two political systems soon escalated into a war in 1840, triggered by Britain's attempt to close its trade deficit with China by exporting opium to China. The war ended with a victory on the bourgeoisie, which represented advanced science, technology and the political system of that time. They chose, after careful consideration, Shanghai as a new mercantile port due to its favorable location in Yangtze River Delta on China's eastern coast and its equidistance between north and south China, which greatly facilitated navigation. As a result, Shanghai was officially opened as a commercial port in 1843.

The raging fire of the Enlightenment Movement has burned in Shanghai ever since.

After making a presence in Shanghai, besides being engaged in business, the bourgeoisie imported all their cultural/social achievements into the city. In agriculture-dominated China, they have exploited a piece of land, allowing them to do anything they wished. To enable "free trade", they started banking, security, insurance, oceanic transportation, oil and other industries. They also developed public facilities in their "Settlements", such as tap water, electric light, telephone, telegram and public health services. They even developed entertainment industries, gambling houses, ballrooms, stage theaters and cinemas.

More importantly, they built Shanghai into a "land of freedom", where the laws of the feudal authority did not apply. They established churches, disseminated contract culture, and advocated a political system of checks and balances. They set up institutions of secondary and higher education such as Saint John's University, for imparting scientific and technological knowledge, which shook the ideological foundation of the feudal and imperial authority of that time in China. As a result, there emerged a division of political philosophies within the country's feudal ruling class. The national bourgeoisie in China initiated in 1861 the Westernization Movement, aiming at self-strengthening. They learned and adopted sophisticated Western techniques and boosted the modern military industry. A notable example was the establishment of the General Bureau of Machine Manufacture of Jiangnan in Shanghai.

After understanding the above-mentioned origin, it is much easier to understand the purpose of those buildings when we reopen this book and put ourselves in Shanghai, the oriental metropolis emerging in the first half of the last century.

End of the preface.

Di Wei
Early Summer, 2014
At Huangpu River

安仁街、北京东路、广东路等
Anren Street, East Beijing Road, Guangdong Road, etc.

九曲桥

（安仁街132号）

　　九曲桥位于豫园内。豫园本是一座私家园林，建于明代。而九曲桥的建造较晚，约于清乾隆年间（1736～1795）。该桥最初是一座木桥，20世纪20年代改建为水泥桥。

Nine Zigzag Bridge
This bridge is located in Yu Garden, previously a private garden built during the Ming Dynasty (1368-1644).
Location: No. 132, Anren Street

格林邮船大楼

(北京东路2号)

　　这是原英商蓝烟囱轮船公司旧址，本名为格林邮船大楼。1951年上海人民广播电台迁入其中，于是人们又习惯于称其为"广播大楼"。

Glen Line Building

The Former British Blue Funnel Line Building housed offices of the Blue Funnel Line. Its original name was Glen Line Building.

Location: No. 2, East Beijing Road

国华商业银行大楼

（北京东路342号）

国华商业银行于1928年在上海成立，原名国华银行，由邹敏初、邓瑞人等创办。其中华侨资本占相当比例，经营商业融资、外汇、信托、储蓄、仓库等业务。1951年起由中国人民银行总行管辖。该大楼于1933年竣工。

Former China State Bank Building

Completed in 1933, the building was the home of China State Bank. It was taken over by the People's Bank of China (PBOC) in 1951.

Location: No. 342, East Beijing Road

益丰洋行

（北京东路31～91号）

这幢建筑前身为益丰洋行。建筑为英商思九生洋行设计，建成于1911年。

Former Abraham E Building
Built in 1911, it used to house the Abraham E, a famous foreign company at that time.
Location: No. 31 to 91, East Beijing Road

四明银行大楼

（北京东路232～240号）

　　1908年四明商业银行在上海成立。1921年迁入这栋新落成的办公大楼。1933年设立四明储蓄会。

Former Building of Siming Bank

The bank came into existence in Shanghai in 1908. The office building was constructed in 1921.
Location: No. 232 to 240, East Beijing Road

雷士德医学院

（北京西路 1314～1320 号）

该建筑系雷士德医学院校舍，1935 年落成开学。建筑风格为现代派。当时该学院规定，主要生源为华人子弟，同时也适当接纳除英、美、法三国以外的其他国籍学生。

Former Henry Lester Institute of Medical Research
This school building of the Henry Lester Institute of Medical Research was opened in 1935.
Location: No. 1314 to 1320, West Beijing Road

[百老汇大厦]

(北苏州路20号)

百老汇大厦因伫立于百老汇路(今大名路)顶端而得名。这是一幢早期现代派风格的建筑,于1934年竣工。

Former Broadway Mansion

Completed in 1934, in a typical style of early modern architecture, it was named after Broadway Road (today's Daming Road) where it was located.
Location: No. 20, North Suzhou Road

上海邮政总局

(北苏州路276号)

该楼始建于1924年,由门厅拾阶而上直接进入的二楼营业大厅,曾被誉为"远东第一大厅"。

Former General Post Office

Its construction began in 1924; the hallway steps lead directly to the operotional hall on the Second floor. It was once renowned as the "best hall in the Far East".

Location: No. 276, North Suzhou Road

大上海博物馆

（长海路174号）

此建筑于1936年建成开放，建筑造型与当时的大上海图书馆类似，当年竣工后在这里首次展出的是中国建筑展览会。

Former Shanghai Museum

Completed and opened to the public in 1936, the building was first used to host the Chinese Architecture Exhibition.
Location: No. 174, Changhai Road

提篮桥监狱

（长阳路147号）

号称"远东第一监狱"的提篮桥监狱是由英国人于1901年开工，1903年落成启用。该监狱是中国仍在使用的历史最悠久的监狱。抗日战争胜利后，提篮桥监狱先后关押过几百名日本战犯，是抗战胜利后中国境内第一次审判日本战犯的法庭所在地。

Tilanqiao Prison

Dubbed the "No.1 Prisonvin the Far East", its construction was started by the British in 1901 and it was opened for operation in 1903. It was used to detain several hundred Japanese war criminals after the Anti-Japanese War.

Location: No. 147, Changyang Road

徐家汇藏书楼

（漕溪北路80号）

现存的徐家汇藏书楼包括两幢建筑："南楼"又称"神父楼"，西式建筑，始建于清同治六年（1867）；"北楼"现称"藏经楼"，当年即为藏书楼，清光绪二十三年（1897）建成。北楼乃当代图书馆之雏形。楼下为中文书库，仿清代《四库全书》文澜阁模式；二楼是西文书库，仿梵蒂冈藏书楼的风格。

Bibliotheca Zikawei

Completed in 1897 with a floor area of over 2,000 m², it was an early form of a contemporary library.
Location: No. 80, North Caoxi Road

震旦大学博物馆

(重庆南路225号)

震旦大学是天主教耶稣会在中国上海创办的教会大学。由中国神父马相伯于1903年在徐家汇天文台旧址创办。1952年全国院系调整,将震旦大学各院系分别归并上海市各有关高等学校。这幢建筑原为震旦大学博物馆,1930年建造。

Museum of Aurora University

Aurora University was a church university established by the Societas Jesus in Shanghai. Completed in 1930, this building was the university's Museum.
Location: No. 225, South Chongqing Road

大千胜境石牌坊

（大境路259号）

　　这座石牌坊建于清道光十六年（1836）。据说，当时的总督陈銮游览至此题写了"大千胜境"四个字，并刻于石坊上。

Archway Gate with Numerous Stones

The structure, also known as Dajingfang Archway, was built in 1836.
Location: No. 259, Dajing Road

南洋兄弟烟草公司

(东大名路817号)

华人简照南、简玉阶兄弟于1905年在香港设立广东南洋烟草公司，1915年来上海开设了上海制烟厂。

Former Nanyang Brothers Tobacco

Zhaonan and Yujie Jian, two Chinese brothers founded the Nanyang Brothers Tobacco Company in Hong Kong in 1905. The company later opened a factory in Shanghai.
Location: No. 817, East Daming Road

耶松船厂

(东大名路388号)

耶松船厂是当年英商在华设立的船舶修造厂,清同治四年(1865)在上海成立。1900年,该船厂与祥生船厂联合,成立耶松船厂公司,1908年建成这幢公司大楼。

Former Shipyard of S.C.
This shipyard was established by S.C. Farnham and Co., a British company; its office building was completed in 1908.
Location: No. 388, East Daming Road

雷士德工学院

(东长治路505号)

英国富商亨利·雷士德逝世后将财产委托上海公共租界工部局管理。工部局成立了雷士德基金会，1933年创办雷士德工学院。1934年奠基落成此建筑。

Former Lester School and Henry Lester Institute of Technical Education

In keeping with arrangements made by Henry Lester (1840–1926), a British merchant, after his death, his assets were to be managed by the Shanghai Municipal Council of the Shanghai International Settlement. After assuming management of his wealth, the council established the Henry Lester Trust Limited that funded the construction of the school in 1933.

Location: No. 505, East Changzhi Road

仁记洋行

(滇池路 100～110 号)

　　原仁记洋行大楼,建造于 1908 年。仁记洋行创办于清道光二十三年(1843),主要经营茶叶、生丝、木材、纸张、五金等进出口业务,是首批抵沪的外资企业。

Former Gibb, Livingston & Co.
The building was completed in 1908.
Location: No. 100 to110, Dianchi Road

业广地产有限公司

(滇池路120号)

　　这幢英式建筑风格大楼，是由通和洋行设计，于1908年竣工，属英商业广地产有限公司所有。该公司以出租房屋为主营，兼做抵押、买卖等商业银行的业务。中国居民和小型工商业主是其房屋出租主要对象。1956年，公司以所有资产转让给中华企业公司而结束了在沪的数十年经营。

Former Landwide Estates Co., Ltd Building
This English-style building was designed by At kinson&Dallas and completed in 1908.
Location: No. 120, Dianchi Road

比利时领事馆

（汾阳路 20 号）

这座具有德国风格的建筑，坐落在上海音乐学院内西南角。其建于 1926 年，1927 年比利时驻沪领事馆在此开馆，1950 年上海音乐学院迁入该址。

Former Consulate General of the Kingdom of Belgium
It was completed in 1926.
Location: No. 20, Fenyang Road

海关俱乐部

(汾阳路9弄3号)

中国海关关署在此址建造了这幢中国海关关署俱乐部,竣工于清光绪二十四年(1898),俗称小木楼。该建筑为现存上海最老的木结构独立式花园洋房之一。

Former Customs Club of China

Completed in 1898, it was built by the Customs Agency of China and referred to as the "Wood House".
Location: No. 3, Lane No. 9, Fenyang Road

美国花旗总会

（福州路209号）

　　1917年，美国侨民设立花旗总会，后在原静安寺路建屋，改称斜桥总会。1923年应一些较有地位的美侨需要，在今址开建了这座花旗总会大楼，于1925年建成。

The Former American Club

It was established in 1917. This American Club Building was built in 1925 at the request of some American Chinese of high social status in 1923.
Location: No. 209, Fuzhou Road

妇产科医院

(方斜路419号)

妇产科医院前身为西门妇孺医院,是一所美国基督教会主办的教会医院。清光绪十年(1884)由美国人玛格丽特·威廉逊女士捐款在上海旧城西门外租房两间,创办门诊部。这幢建筑约建于20世纪30年代。

Former Obstetrics & Gynecology Hospital

The Hospital of Fudan University (or Shanghai Red House Obstetrics&Gynecology Hospital), formerly the Margaret Williamson Hospital, was a church hospital established by American Christians. This building was constructed in the 1930s.
Location: No. 419, Fang Xie Road

同济德文医学工学堂图书馆

（复兴中路1195号）

上海理工大学即原同济德文医工学堂。1920年被中法两国政府定名为"上海中法国立通惠工商学校"。该校图书馆建于1916年，是上海唯一一栋普鲁士风格的建筑。

Former Deutsche Ingenieurschule Library

It is now in the University of Shanghai for Science and Technology. Built in 1916, the library was the only one of Prussian style in Shanghai.

Location: No. 1195, Middle Fuxing Road

日清轮船公司

（广东路20号）

这幢大楼，由德和洋行设计，始建于1921年，1925年落成，为原日清汽船株式会社的办公大楼。该株式会社是日商于1907年组建的一家股份制轮船公司。

Former Japan-China Steamship Company

This building, completed in 1925, was the former office building of the Japan-China Steamship Co. in Shanghai.

Location: No. 20, Guangdong Road

永年人寿保险公司

（广东路93号）

该建筑由英国人创办的永年人寿保险公司出资，于1910年建造。建筑的主要部分于1913年被三北轮船公司买下，故又称"三北轮船公司大楼"。

Former Yongnian Life Insurance Company
Built in 1910, by Yongnian Life Insurance Company.
Location: No. 93, Guangdong Road

> 三菱洋行

（广东路102号）

此楼出自日本建筑师的设计，建于1912年，系三菱洋行的办公楼。

Former Mitsubishi Company
Designed by a Japanese architect and built in 1912, it housed the offices of the Mitsubishi Co.
Location: No. 102, Guangdong Road

| 中央造币厂 |

（光复西路17号）

上海银行公会于1920年提议，经北洋政府批准，这栋上海造币厂大楼破土动工。1930年春，上海中央造币厂成立。

Former Central Mint

This classical European building of the Central Mint, formerly the Shanghai Mint was proposed by the Shanghai Bankers' Association and approved by the Beiyang Warlord Government (1912-1928).
Location: No. 17, West Guangfu Road

江南造船厂

（高雄路 2 号）

　　江南造船厂始建于清同治四年（1865）。据悉，仅至 1949 年，该厂就建造了各类舰船 884 艘。这幢机装车间建于 20 世纪 30 年代。

Former Jiangnan Shipyard
The shipyard was established in 1865 during the Self-Strengthening Movement in the late 19th century during the Qing Dynasty (1644-1911). This tool workshop was built in the 1930s.
Location: No. 2, Gaoxiong Road

江湾体育场

（国和路346号）

　　此建筑于1935年投入使用，是当时远东最大的综合性体育场馆。1983年的第五届全国运动会即是在这里举行的。

Former Jiangwan Stadium
Coming into service in 1935, the building was the largest comprehensive stadium in the Far East.
Location: No. 346, Guohe Road

美国学校

(华山路639号)

　　这幢建筑原是一所美国学校,为钢筋混凝土结构,于1941年竣工。1947年宋庆龄在此创办了中国福利会儿童福利院。

Former American School

It was a building of an American school, finished in 1941. In 1947, Soong Ching-ling, the second wife of Sun Yat-sen, founded the Children Welfare Office of China Welfare Institute (CWI) here.

Location: No. 639, Huashan Road

中国福利会儿童艺术剧院

（华山路643号）

这幢建筑竣工于1937年。1947年，宋庆龄女士在此创办了中国福利会儿童艺术剧院。

Children's Theatre of China Welfare Institute (CWI)

The building was completed in 1937. Madame Soong Ching-ling, the second wife of Sun Yat-sen, the founder of the Republic of China (1911-1949) founded the Institute in 1947.

Location: No. 643, Huashan Road

南洋公学图书馆

(华山路 1954 号)

　　南阳公学图书馆是由南洋公学 1916 级毕业班同学为纪念建校 20 周年，向社会各界及师生共同募资建造的。建筑于 1919 年竣工。

Former Nan Yang Public School Library

Completed in 1919, this building was constructed with funds raised by the graduating class of 1916 of the Nan Yang Public School to mark its 20th anniversary. The funds were from faculty, students and people from all walks of life.

Location: No. 1954, Huashan Road

中法学堂

（淮海东路70号）

　　光明中学创建于清光绪十二年（1886），原名"法文书馆"。当时，这所学校是用于教授华人学习法语的，因而学杂费及书籍全免。1911年改称"中法学堂"。学校成立几经迁徙，于1913年迁至今址，并建造了这幢建筑。

Former Sino-French School

A predecessor of the Shanghai GuangMing High School, it moved to this site in 1913 and this building was constructed later.

Location: No. 70, East Huaihai Road

恩派亚大戏院

(淮海中路 85 号)

　　1921 年由葡萄牙人雷玛斯创建，"恩派亚"一名为葡语 Empire 的音译。1926 年出租给中央影戏公司经营电影放映。两年后转由美商经营，1935 年起由国人接手，始有地方戏曲演出。1951 年因其近嵩山路而改名嵩山戏院。20 世纪 90 年代因淮海路改造而被拆除。

Empire Theater
The theater, made of brick and wood, was established by a Portuguese investor in 1921; it was renamed Songshan Theater in 1951 because of its proximity to Songshan Road.
Location: No. 85, Middle Huaihai Road

国泰大戏院

(淮海中路870号)

该戏院由匈牙利建筑师设计,1932年竣工,是当年上海滩装潢最为富丽、音响效果最佳的影剧院之一。

Former Cathay Theatre

Formerly known as the Cathay Theatre, the Cathay Cinema was designed by a Hungarian architect and completed in 1932. It was renowned as one of the theatres with the best acoustics and most luxurious decorations.

Location: No. 870, Middle Huaihai Road

法租界巡捕房

（淮海中路235号）

这幢法国文艺复兴风格的建筑建于1914年。1921年10月4日，陈独秀被上海法租界巡捕房逮捕，即关押于此。

Former Municipal Police, French Concession

Built in 1914, it is typical French Renaissance style.

Location: No. 235, Middle Huaihai Road

法租界公董局

(淮海中路381号)

　　这幢建筑于1909年落成,1911年起成为一所法国小学,后又改作法国军队的兵营。1936年法国公董局迁入其中。

Former Conseil D'Administration Municipale de la Concession Française de Shanghai

Completed in 1909, the building housed the Conseil D'Administration Municipale since 1936. It is a classical late French Renaissance style on the Bund.

Location: No. 381, Middle Huaihai Road

礼查饭店

(黄浦路 15 号)

　　1846 年,英国商人阿斯脱豪夫·礼查兴建礼查饭店。1856 年,将礼查饭店从原址迁移至此。然因当时地处偏僻,饭店经营状况欠佳。1860 年,英国人史密斯接手经营,改名为 Astor House,并在原客房业务的基础又开设了弹子房、酒吧、舞厅及牌室,饭店经营日益繁荣。1907 年饭店扩建,成为当时上海最豪华的西商饭店。爱因斯坦、卓别林、罗素、美国前总统格兰特等名人皆曾客宿于此。

Former British Richard Astor House
In 1846, an English businessman built Richard's Hotel and Restaurant. In 1856, the restaurant was renovated.
Location: No. 15, Huangpu Road

俄罗斯领事馆

(黄浦路20号)

　　这幢红顶白壁别墅，建于1916年，1924年成为苏联驻上海的总领事馆，后成为俄罗斯驻上海总领事馆。

Consulate General of Russia

Built in 1916, this villa with red roof and white walls housed the Shanghai Consulate General of the Soviet Union and later of Russia.
Location: No. 20, Huangpu Road

上海储能中学一分部

（黄陂南路25号乙）

上海储能中学创建于1942年，曾以"民主革命堡垒，爱国志士摇篮"享誉沪上。此建筑建造年代不详。据悉，当初"颜料大王"贝润生于1911年购得，按照苏州园林风格整修，于是楼房与周边环境形成了中西合璧之妙。该建筑于2001年市政改建时被拆除。

A Part of the Former Shanghai Chunneng Middle School

It's unclear when it was constructed. It was purchased by Bei Runsheng, a paint businessman renowned as the "King of Paint" in 1911. He renovated the building with reference to the Suzhou Garden. Consequently, the building and its surroundings have both Chinese and Western appeal.

Location: Building B, No. 25, South Huangpi Road

| 虹口大旅社 |

（海宁路449号）

　　该建筑亦称虹口大楼，1927年建成。抗日战争期间，南部一部分曾被战火毁坏，且整幢大楼被日军占据。今天的虹口大楼，上层为民居，底层为百货商店。

Former Hongkou Hotel
Completed in 1927, it is a seven-story Art Deco style building.
Location: No. 449, Haining Road

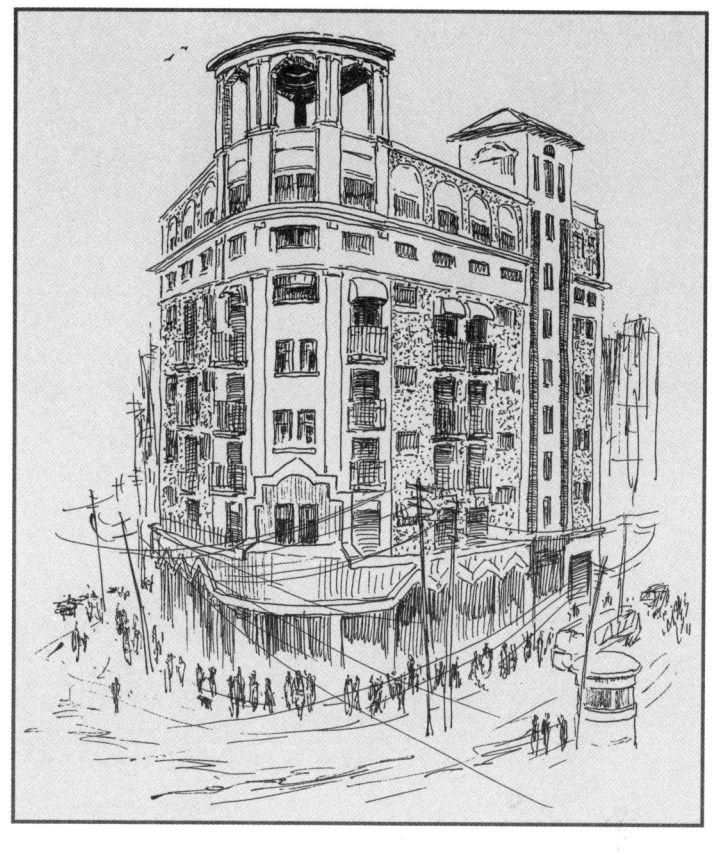

浙江第一商业银行

（汉口路151号）

　　1909年浙江银行成立，总行设在杭州。次年在沪开设上海分行。1940年，银行选址于此拟建造银行大楼。然而打桩后的建筑工程因战乱停建。抗战胜利后，改名为浙江省银行的上海分行于1947年恢复。次年银行改名为浙江第一商业银行，并决定复建银行大楼。大楼直到1951年才竣工。

Former Chekiang Commercial Bank

The Bank of Chekiang established a Shanghai branch in 1910, and chose this site to construct a new bank building in 1940.
Location: No. 151, Hankou Road

| 公共租界工部局 |

(汉口路193号)

　　这幢大楼建于1919年，是当年上海公共租界最高行政机构——工部局的办公楼。

Former Municipal Council of the Shanghai International Settlement

Built in 1919, it is the office building of the Municipal Council, the highest administrative institution in the Shanghai Public Settlement.

Location: No. 193, Hankou Road

《申报》报馆

（汉口路309号）

　　《申报》馆大楼建于1918年。当年，大楼底层为铸字、排字、纸型、铅板、铜锌版乃至印刷场所；以上楼层则是营业、编辑、校对、照相、办公、图书馆等工作空间。上海《申报》是我国近代创办较早、历时最久的报纸，创刊于清同治十一年（1872），1949年停刊。

Former Building of the Shanghai News

Built in 1918, this neoclassical style, building housed offices of the *Shen Bao*, or *Shanghai News* newspaper.

Location: No. 309, Hankou Road

美童公学

（衡山路 10 号）

　　这幢建筑建于 1922 年，主楼由美国建筑师亨利·墨菲设计，是以教会为背景的美童公学所在地。

Former Shanghai American School
Built in 1922, it has a style similar to the American Independence Hall. It was a school for American children.
Location: No. 10, Hengshan Road

亚洲文会北中国支会

（虎丘路20号）

英国侨民于清咸丰七年（1857）在上海建立亚洲文会北中国支会，清同治十年（1871）在此址建造会所。1931年拆旧重建，1932年建成这座中西结合风格的杰作。

Former Site of the North China Branch of the Royal Asiatic Society

In 1857, British nationals established the North China Branch of the Royal Asiatic Society in Shanghai. In 1871, an office building of the branch was constructed on this site.

Location: No. 20, Huqiu Road

光陆大戏院

（虎丘路142号）

　　光陆大戏院位于光陆大楼的底部两层。该大楼共八层，除戏院外，以上均为写字楼和公寓。其由英商斯文洋行投资，匈牙利籍建筑师鸿达设计，1928年落成，是上海最先将剧场置于大楼之内的建筑。1953年改名曙光剧场，1982年改为上海国际贸易会堂。

Former Capitol Theatre

Completed in 1928 on the first and second floor of the Capitol Building, it was the first in-doors theatre in Shanghai.
Location: No. 142, Huqiu Road

商船会馆

（会馆街38号）

商船会馆是上海最早的一座会馆。该会馆由商船运输业中的沙船业主们于清康熙五十四年（1715）集资建造，是以本帮沙船业为主的同业会所。清道光年间（1821～1850），这个会馆在上海各会馆中的地位达到了顶峰。

Former Merchant Shipping Guildhall

This guildhall was built by the owners of large junks and Chinese sailboats in the shipping industry by pooling their money in 1715. It was the earliest building of its kind in Shanghai.

Location: No. 38, Huiguan Street

徐汇公学崇思楼

（虹桥路50号）

　　徐汇公学的崇思楼由比利时神父、建筑师第斯尼设计，并监督建造，1917年奠基，1918落成，现坐落于徐汇中学内。

Former Chongsi Building of the Xuhui Public School

It was designed by Disney, a Belgian priest and architect, who also supervised its construction. Its foundation laid in 1917, the building was completed in 1918. It is now in Xuhui High School.

Location: No. 50, Hongqiao Road

九江路、浦东南路、四川路等
Jiujiang Road, South Pudong Road, Sichuan Road, etc.

原德华银行旧址

（九江路89号）

　　这幢江川大楼原为德华银行所在地，1916年建成。德华银行于清光绪十五年（1889）在上海成立，由德国13家大银行联合投资组成，系当时德国资本在中国运作的中心。

Former Site of Deutsche Asiatische Bank

Completed in 1916, the Jiangchuan Building used to house the Deutsche Asiatische Bank.

Location: No. 89, Jiujiang Road

沪江大学图书馆

（军工路516号）

美国南、北浸信会于1906在上海创办浸信会神学院，于1909年又开设浸信会大学堂。1911年两部分合并组建上海浸信会大学。1914年，该大学改名为沪江大学。这座沪江大学图书馆建造于1928年。

Former Library of Shanghai University

The American Baptist Missionary Union and the Southern Baptist Convention in Shanghai established the Shanghai Baptist Theological Seminary in 1906 and the Shanghai Baptist College in 1909. The two were combined in 1911 to form Shanghai Baptist College and Theological Seminary, which changed its name to the University of Shanghai in 1914. This building was completed in 1928.

Location: No. 516, Jungong Road

美琪大戏院

（江宁路66号）

美琪大戏院建于1941年，风格为近代美国式。该建筑在上海近代建筑史中有着突出的地位，反映了当时的建筑设计和营造水平。

The Majestic Theatre
In the modern American architecture style, it was completed in 1941.
Location: No. 66, Jiangning Road

中西女塾

（江苏路155号）

　　市三女中的前身是美国人于清光绪十八年（1892）创办的教会中学——中西女塾，1917年迁址于此。1929年中西女塾向中国政府立案，聘请杨锡珍为第一任华人校长。1930年改名为中西女中。宋氏三姐妹曾就读于此。教学楼景莲堂建于1935年，属哥特复兴式美国学院派风格。

Former McTyeire School

McTyeire School, where the Soong Sisters Studied (Soong E. Ling, Song Ching Ling, Soong May Ling), established by Americans in 1892, is now the Shanghai No.3 Girls' High School. The school moved here in 1917.

Location: No. 155, Jiangsu Road

礼和洋行大楼

(江西中路255号)

　　德商礼和洋行（又名卡洛威茨公司）是德商在中国创办最早的洋行之一。此楼为该洋行的办公楼，建成于1898年。1927年后，新华商业储蓄银行上海分行租赁该大楼底层部分空间用于营业，于是也有人称之为"新华银行大楼"。

Former Building of Carlowitz & Co.
Built in 1898, it was the office building of Carlowitz & Co. (AKA Carlowitz Harkort &Co.)
Location: No. 255, Middle Jiangxi Road

汉弥尔登大楼

（江西中路170号）

汉弥尔登大楼当年由公和洋行设计，新仁记营造厂施工。1933年落成后，大楼即作为写字楼和公寓出租，不少著名海外企业和机构纷纷入驻。其中不乏福特汽车公司、可口可乐公司、美国新闻处等著名企业和重要办事处。1959年该建筑改名为福州大楼。

Former Hamilton House

Since 1933, when the building was completed, it was rented as an office building as well as an apartment. Many famous overseas enterprises and institutions set up offices here.

Location: No. 170, Middle Jiangxi Road

建设大厦

（江西中路181号）

此大厦本为中国通商银行新楼，1934年开建。1935年因资金紧缺，原建造者只得将之卖给中国建设银公司，故大楼名为建设大厦。大厦于1936年竣工。

The Construction Building

It was resold to China Development Finance Corporation as an unfinished building of Commercial Bank of China, thus being named the Construction Building.

Location: No. 181, Middle Jiangxi Road

清心女中

(陆家浜路650号)

原上海市市八女中前身是清心书院，于清咸丰十年（1860）创办，该建筑于1933年建成。1918年改制为清心女子中学，1953年改为上海市第八女子中学。

Former Mary Farnham Girls' School
The Mary Farnham Academy, the predecessor of the Shanghai No.8 Girls' High School, was established by John Farnham, an American Presbyterian missionary, and his wife. In 1918, it was restructured and renamed Mary Farnham Girls' School.
Location: No. 650, Lujiabang Road

英侨业余戏剧协会剧场

（茂名南路57号）

今兰心大戏院原本属英桥上海业余剧社兰心大戏院保管会，当时主要演出话剧兼放电影，1931年落成。

Former British-Chinese Amateur Drama Club

Today's Lyceum Theatre was under the Custody Association of the Shanghai British-Chinese Amateur Drama Club, which staged plays and films at that time.

Location: No. 57, South Maoming Road

永安公司大楼

（南京路627号）

　　永安公司于1907年由原在澳大利亚悉尼经营水果批发的华侨郭标、郭乐、郭泉在香港创办。1918年，该公司在上海创办永安百货。永安公司大楼是中国早期建筑综合体的典范。在20世纪30年代，即已集中了大型百货、茶楼、酒店、舞厅和溜冰场于一身。

Former Wing On Department Store

Completed in 1933, this building best represented the early Chinese building complexes.

Location: No. 627, Nanjing Road

汇中饭店

(南京东路23号)

　　这座竣工于1908年的建筑,原为汇中饭店,亦名中央饭店。1909年"万国禁烟会"就在这里举行。1911年中国同盟本部在该饭店召开了孙中山就任临时大总统欢迎大会。该建筑现为和平饭店南楼。

Former Palace Hotel

Completed in 1908, this American-style building is known as the Palace Hotel or the Central Hotel. In 1909, the first meeting of the World Anti-Narcotics League was held here. In 1911, it was here the Chinese United League congratulated Sun Yat-sen on serving as interim president.

Location: No. 23, East Nanjing Road

上海电力公司大楼

(南京东路181号)

上海电力公司大楼于1929年落成。上海电力公司最早由英国人创办，名为上海电光公司，是中国第一家电气经营企业。

Former Building of Shanghai Power Company

It was completed in 1929 by the British. Location: No. 181, East Nanjing Road

先施公司

（南京东路690号）

　　这幢大厦是1915年破土动工，由顾兰记营造厂承建，1917年竣工，是上海先施公司旧址。

The Former Sincere Company

Completed in 1917, it used to be the home of Sincere Company.

Location: No. 690, East Nanjing Road

慈昌大厦

（南京东路98～114号）

　　慈安里大楼原名慈昌大厦，建于1906年。1934年外商合资经营的大型百货商店福利公司迁址于此，1955年停业。

Former Cichang Building
Ci'anli Building, formally known as Cichang Building, was built in 1906.
Location: No. 98 to114, East Nanjing Road

新新公司

（南京东路720号）

　　新新公司本是南京路"四大公司"中第三家新开张的大公司。这幢大楼由匈牙利建筑师鸿达设计，香港联益营造厂承建，建造于1925年。

The Former Sun Sun Company
Built in 1925, it was then one of the "top four" department stores on Nanjing Road.
Location: No. 720, East Nanjing Road

> 大新公司

（南京东路830号）

　　1932年，澳大利亚华侨蔡昌来到上海决定在新新公司西侧，开设一家新的百货公司——大新公司，公司大楼于1936年竣工。该建筑在国内首创地下商场，配备了连贯直达三楼的自动扶梯。大新公司虽然是华人所开"四大公司"最后一家，但却后来居上，成为龙头。

Former Sun Co., Ltd
Completed in 1936, it housed the Sun Company, a department store set up by an Australian Chinese businessman.
Location: No. 830, East Nanjing Road

新世界游乐场

(南京西路1号)

此址原是旧上海早期的大型游乐场——新世界。1915年由黄楚九、经润三创办，1916年竣工。内设崖顶花园、茶室、餐厅、游戏室、影戏场等。1993年，新世界游乐场因南京路改造被拆除。

Former New World Amusement Arcade
Completed in 1916, it was a major amusement arcade in Shanghai before the founding of the PRC
Location: No.1, West Nanjing Road

华安人寿保险公司

(南京西路104号)

华安大楼由华安合群人寿保险公司建造。华安公司几经搬迁，于1922年买下今址地块，投资建造了这幢华安合群人寿保险公司大楼，并于1926年建成。1939年，大楼被一香港华侨租下，并更名为金门大酒店，成为上海滩的一家知名酒店。

Former Building of Hua'an Life Insurance Company
It was built by Hua'an Hequn Life Insurance Company and completed in 1926.
Location: No. 104, West Nanjing Road

四行储蓄会大楼

（南京西路170号）

今国际饭店，本是一家名为"四行储蓄汇"的银行，该建筑当初也叫"四行储蓄会大楼"。由于该建筑1934年竣工后，曾在长达半个多世纪里稳居东亚第一高度，故获有"远东第一楼"之美誉。该建筑曾经历"派克饭店""花园饭店"等经营历程，今为国际饭店。

Former Building for the Savings Society of Four Banks

Completed in 1934, it was the tallest structure in the East Asia for more than half a century.

Location: No. 170, West Nanjing Road

大光明电影院

（南京西路216号）

享有"远东第一影院"盛名的大光明电影院，始建于1928年，由中国商人高永清和美国华纳兄弟电影公司创始人亚伯特·华纳合资建造。影院开张时，京剧大师梅兰芳亲自为之剪彩。

Shanghai Ever-Shining Circuit Cinema

It long held a reputation as the best cinema in the Far East. Construction started in 1928; it was the first cinema in Asia equipped with wide screen and stereo system.

Location: No. 216, West Nanjing Road

跑马总会

（南京西路325号）

　　这幢建筑于1933年建成。上海自1850年即开始出现跑马赛事，当年由麒瑞洋行的大班、英国人霍格等五人组成了上海最早的"跑马总会"。跑马场几经挪动，后来西移到了今天这个位置。

Former Race Club

It is where the Shanghai Race Course was located over a century ago. This bell-tower shaped building was completed in 1933.

Location: No. 325, West Nanjing Road

> 犹太人总会

（南京西路702～722号）

上海犹太人总会又称"犹太商会"，建于1911年。其原本是上海巨商、爱国人士叶澄衷之子叶贻铨的私宅。

Former Jewish Club

Built in 1911, it was also called the Jewish Chamber of Commerce.
Location: No. 702 to 722, West Nanjing Road

[同孚大楼]

(南京西路801～803号)

　　这栋同孚大楼,约建于1935年,属于现代式建筑。该楼是民国时期中国银行出于自用需要而建。

Yates Apartments

The modern architectural style building was completed in 1935.

Location: No. 801 to 803, West Nanjing Road

[法童学堂]

(南昌路47号)

　　1917年，法国总会投资建造了这幢法国古典花园楼宇。1926年，法国总会迁走，将这里捐给了法国学堂。该学堂以接收法侨和其他外侨子女就读为主，故该建筑又称法童学堂。1958年，此处正式归科学协会使用，更名为科学会堂。

Former Shanghai French School

Built by the French General Assembly, it was donated to the French School in 1926 for educating French children and those from other foreign countries, thus also named Shanghai French School.

Location: No. 47, Nanchang Road

法国总会

（南昌路57号）

这座法国文艺复兴风格的建筑，系20世纪30年代当地上层名流出没的娱乐场所。据说当年舞厅安装了"弹簧地板"，舞者足下可感受到柔韧的弹性。1949年以后这里成为上海市政府管辖的文化俱乐部。

Former College Francais

In French Renaissance style, the college served as an entertainment venue for celebrities in the 1930s.
Location: No. 57, Nanchang Road

英美颐中烟草股份有限公司

（南苏州路 161～175 号）

　　成立于 1902 年的英美烟公司为扩大其在世界范围内的业务需要，于 1919 年联袂来华，决定投资设立驻华英美烟有限公司，并将总部设在此址，统管英美烟公司在华生产及经营业务。1920 年该公司大楼落成。

Former British-American YeeTsoong Tobacco Co.,Ltd
The building was completed in 1920. British American Tobacco established a branch headquarter here.
Location: No. 161 to 175, South Suzhou Road

上海特别市政府

(平江路 48 号)

这组建筑建于 1919 年,最初的主人是江苏对外交涉使公署,1927 年上海特别市政府入驻。1933 年,上海特别市政府迁往江湾新大楼办公,这里又被民国政府外交部上海办事处使用。

Former Special Municipal Government of Shanghai

The complex was built in 1919, housing Shanghai Special Government from 1927 to 1933.

location: No. 48, Pingjiang Road

上海天文台

（蒲西路 166 号）

　　法国天主教会于清同治十一年（1872）在上海建立天文台，此建筑为 1901 年建成的新台址。

Shanghai Astronomical Observatory

In 1872, French Jesuits in Shanghai established the Zikawei Observatory, predecessor of the Shanghai Astronomical Observatory. This building was completed in 1901 when the observatory was relocated here.

Location: No. 166, Puxi Road

上海证券交易所

（浦东南路528号）

上海证券交易所的这幢大楼是本书中唯一的一幢现代建筑。将之收入其中，一方面是希望读者能够注意到，在上海这块被誉为"万国建筑博览会"的土地上，时下建筑的风格已发生了翻天覆地的变化；另一方面也是希望通过视觉形象的对比，让读者直观地感受到建筑美学的走势。上海证券交易所成立于1990年，归属于中国证监会。这幢办公大楼建于1993年，1997年正式启用。

Shanghai Stock Exchange

Built in 1993 and put into service in 1997, it is the only modern building in this book.
Location: No. 528, South Pudong Road

上海市政府（民国）

（清源环路650号）

　　这幢大厦于1933年落成，采用了中国传统建筑形式，是20世纪30年代中国建筑师设计的代表性作品。

Fomer Municipal Government of Shanghai

Completed in 1933, the building was typical of traditional Chinese architecture, best representing Chinese architects' achievements in the 1930s.

Location: No. 650, Qingyuan Ring Road

> 广慈医院

（瑞金二路197号）

　　广慈医院于1907年由法国天主教会创办。20世纪初，法国人姚宗李任江南传教区主教时，拟创办一所包含外科治疗的西医医院，获法国教会同意。1904年医院开始筹建，4幢两层楼房首先建成。

Former St. Marie Hospital

St. Marie Hospital (Hospital Sainte-Marie in French) was established by French Jesuits in 1907.
Location: No.197, Ruijing Road Number Two

沪宁铁路总公司大楼

(四川路126弄5～21号)

沪宁铁路总公司大楼于1911年建成。大楼由通和洋行设计,元芳洋行建造,系文艺复兴建筑风格。

Former Office Building of the Shanghai and Nanjing Railway Company
Completed in 1911, it is Reraissance style.
Location: No. 5 to 21, Lane No.126, Sichuan Road

商务印书馆

（四川北路856号）

原商务印书馆虹口分店旧址，1923年建造，1925年正式启用。1927年10月鲁迅定居虹口后，多次前往这里购阅书籍。1982年陈云来上海视察，特为商务印书馆虹口分店题词。

Former Commercial Press Building
Officially opened in 1925, it housed the Hongkou Branch of the Commercial Press.
Location: No. 856, North Sichuan Road

中国银行虹口大楼

（四川北路894号）

这幢中国银行虹口大楼，1958年改名为中行大楼。由民国中国银行上海分行投资建造，1932年竣工。转角底部两层为营业大厅，上部为公寓。

Former Hongkou Branch of the Bank of China

Completed in 1932, the building was funded by the Bank of China, Shanghai Branch during the Republic of China.

Location: No. 894, North Sichuan Road

企业大楼

（四川中路33号）

该楼当年是由中国企业银行投资，法国哈沙德洋行设计，昌升营造厂承建，1931年落成的。建筑整体属于装饰艺术派风格。中国企业银行的创办人刘鸿生不仅是一位银行家，而且还是一位爱国企业家。当年为遏制西洋火柴垄断中国的局面，开办民族火柴工业。企业大楼启用后，除底楼为银行外，二至五楼分别为水泥、火柴、毛纺、码头等不同企业的经营场所。刘鸿生本人亦居住办公于其中。

Former Enterprise Building

Funded by the Business Bank of China, its construction was completed in 1931.

Location: No. 33, Middle Sichuan Road

美孚洋行大楼

（四川中路109号）

此建筑为原美孚洋行下属火油公司的办公大楼，1920年建成，系一幢新古典主义风格的建筑。

Former Standard-Vacuum Oil Building

Completed in 1920, it housed the Asiatic Petroleum Co. under the Former Standard-Vacuum Oil Company

Location: No. 109, Middle Sichuan Road

卜内门洋碱有限公司办公楼

（四川中路133号）

　　这幢颇具古典韵味的大楼系原英商卜内门洋碱有限公司总部大楼，建造于1922年。专门经营化学商品的进出口业务，长期垄断旧中国肥田粉、碱类等物资的进口。

Former Office Building of the British Brunner, Mond & Co., Ltd

Built in 1922, this building with classical appeal housed the headquarters of the British Brunner, Mond & Co., Ltd.

Location: No. 133, Middle Sichuan Road

| 三井物产公司上海支店 |

（四川中路175号）

　　这栋建筑建于1903年，是三井物产公司上海支店旧址，此店是日商三井财团在华的分支机构。

Former Mitsui Bussan Kaisha Co.,Ltd, Shanghai Branch

Completed in 1903, it was home to Mitsui Bussan Kaisha Limited Company, Shanghai branch, under the Japanese Mitsui Business Group.
Location: No. 175, Middle Sichuan Road

汇丰大楼

(四川中路220号)

这幢建筑原为新汇丰大楼,为汇丰银行业务的辅助场所,故亦有小汇丰大楼之称。大楼1928年竣工,是一幢以简约新古典主义风格为主的建筑。

New Building of the Hong Kong and Shanghai Banking Corporation (HSBC)
Completed in 1928, it was the New Building of HSBC. Used by the bank as an auxiliary site for banking, it was nicknamed the "Small HSBC Building".
Location: No. 220, Middle Sichuan Road

四行储蓄大楼

（四川中路261号）

四行储蓄大楼，是由当时盐业、金城、中南、大陆四家银行联合设立的四行储蓄会投资建造，于1926年落成。1949年，四行信托部改组为联合商业储蓄信托银行后亦在此办公，故也被称作"联合大楼"。

Former Building for the Saving Society of Four Banks on Hankou Road

Completed in 1926, it was funded by the Savings Society of Four Banks.

Location: No. 261, Sichuan Middle Road

东亚银行大楼

（四川中路299号）

此楼于1927年落成，是香港东亚银行上海分支所在地。

Former Building of the Shanghai Branch of the Bank of East Asia

Completed in 1927, it housed the bank of East Asia, Shanghai Branch.

Location: No. 299, Middle Sichuan Road

里白渡桥

（四川路越过苏州河处）

清光绪四年（1878）租界地工部局建造，名为里白渡桥，亦称白大桥。1923年改建为钢筋混凝土结构。

Libaidu Bridge

In 1878, the Shanghai Municipal Council erected a wooden bridge named Baidu Bridge. After two restorations, the old one was finally replaced by the current reinforced concrete bridge.
Location: Over Suzhou Creek, Sichuan Road

外白渡桥

(苏州河入黄浦江口)

外白渡桥位于苏州河入黄浦江口附近,1907年建成,系全国第一座全钢结构铆接桥梁,亦当今中国唯一留存的不等高桁架结构式桥梁。

Waibaidu Bridge

Also known as the Garden Bridge of Shanghai, it was built in 1907, as the first riveted all-steel bridge in China.
Location: Confluence of Huangpu River and Suzhou Creek

三山会馆

(淞园路15号)

三山会馆是上海唯一保存完好的晚清会馆建筑,始建于1909年,1914年建成。

Sanshan Guildhall

Built in 1914, it is the only well-preserved guildhall of the late Qing Dynasty (1644-1911) remaining in Shanghai.

Location: No. 15, Songyuan Road

新亚大酒楼

（天潼路422号）

　　新亚大酒楼，是由当年五和洋行的英国建筑师席拉设计，桂兰记营造厂承造。建筑约1933年落成。1934年1月新亚大酒楼开业，乃当时沪上高级旅社之一。

The Former Shanghai New Asia Hotel

Designed by an English architect who designed the Republic Land Investment Co., it was completed in around 1933 in the American modern style.

Location: No. 422, Tiantong Road

沪宁铁路上海站（北站）大楼

（天目东路200号）

沪宁铁路上海站于1908年4月开始建造，次年7月竣工，取名沪宁车站。主体建筑为英国古典主义风格，集售票、候车、办公于一体。1916年12月，沪宁、沪杭铁路接轨，沪宁铁路上海站成为两铁路总站，改名上海北站。

Former Shanghai Station (Shanghai North Station) of the Shanghai-Nanjing Railway
Started in 1908 and completed in July 1909, it was firstly named Huning (meaning Shanghai to Nanjing) Station.
Location: No. 200, East Tianmu Road

西区污水处理厂泵房

（天山路 30 号）

　　西区污水处理厂是 1922 年公共租界工部局置地建造的，1926 年完工。西区污水处理厂采用二级活性污泥法处理污水。

The Former Pump House of the West District Sewage Treatment Plant
Built by the Shanghai Municipal Council, it was completed in 1926.
Location: No. 30, Tianshan Road

三角地菜场

(塘沽路 250 号)

　　清光绪十八年(1892)由工部局出资修建了虹口菜场,俗称三角地菜场。1913～1914 年改造,在原址上重建了这座上下三层的钢筋混凝土菜场。该菜场在上海旧城改造时被拆除。

Former Delta Grocery Market

The Hongkou Grocery Market, commonly known as the Delta Grocery Market, was funded and built by the Shanghai Municipal Councilin 1892.
Location: No. 250, Tanggu Road

圣约翰大学办公楼

（万航渡路 1575 号）

　　圣约翰大学是一所在中国办学时间最久的教会学校，清光绪五年（1879）创建之初为圣约翰书院，1905 年改为大学，是中国近代最著名的大学之一，该校毕业生的影响力甚至改变了中国乃至世界近现代的政治、金融、商业等诸多领域的历史。1952 年，圣约翰大学被分拆至上海各大名校后解散，圣约翰大学原校址归属华东政法大学。

Office Building of Saint John's University

The university was one of the oldest and most prestigious missionary universities in China. It was founded in 1879 as St. John's College and became a university in 1905.
Location: No. 1575, Wanhangdu Road

圣约翰大学思颜堂

（万航渡路 1575 号）

　　"思颜堂"是为纪念圣约翰大学创办初期出力最多的颜永京牧师而命名，1904 年落成。该楼呈现 U 字型，采用中西结合建筑形式。

Siyan Hall of Saint John's University

Completed in 1904, it was built in memory of Yan Yongjing, a priest who contributed enormously to Saint John's University during its early days.
Location: No. 1575, Wanhangzhou Road

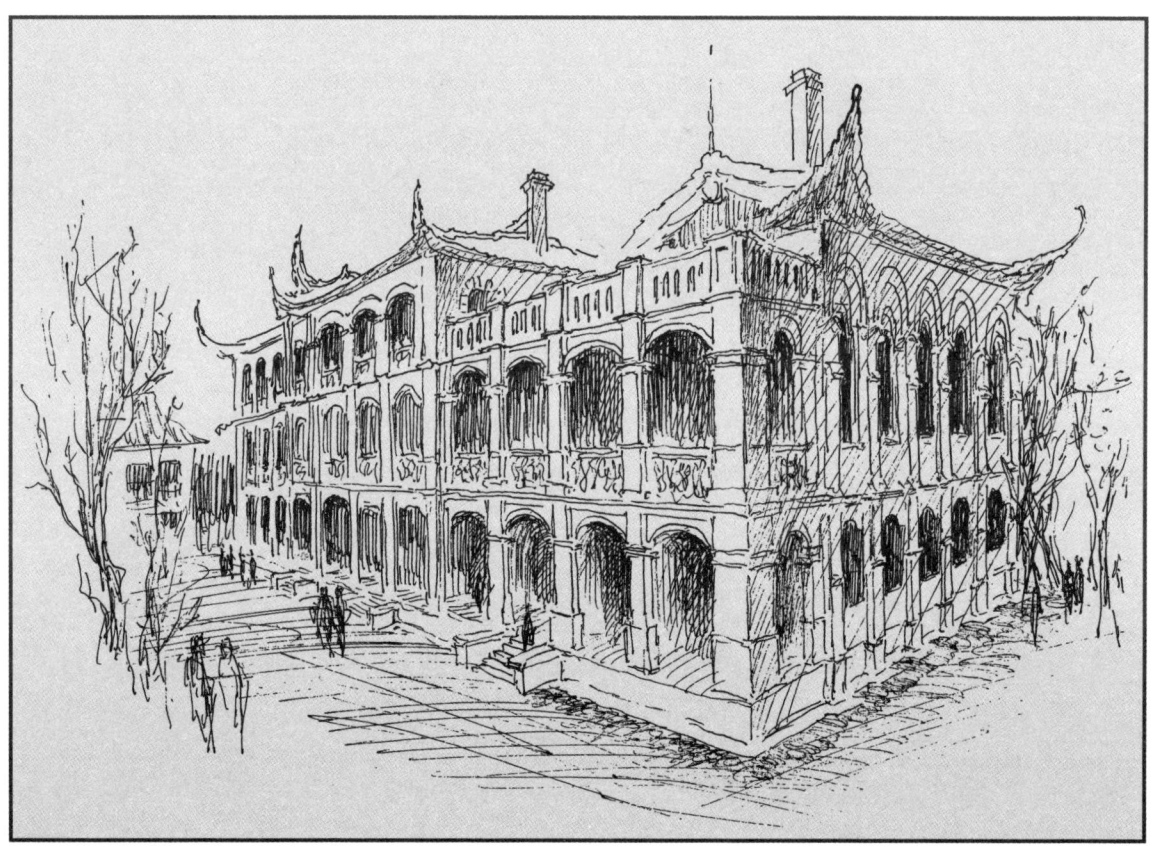

圣约翰大学韬奋楼

（万航渡路 1575 号）

韬奋楼原名怀施堂，系为纪念圣约翰大学创始人施勒楚斯基而命名。新中国成立后，为纪念1921年毕业生邹韬奋改称韬奋楼。

Taofen Building of Saint John's University

It was originally named Schereschewsky Hall in honor of S.I.J.Schereschewsky, the founder of the Saint John's University. After the PRC was founded, it was renamed Taofen Building in honor of Zou Taofen, a 1921 alumnus.

Location: No. 1575, Wanhangdu Road

圣约翰大学体育室

（万航渡路1575号）

圣约翰大学体育室前身为简陋健身房，于1919年落成典礼。1925年举行的远东运动大会全国预选大会在此进行。1952～1956年，华东体育学院曾设于此。

Stadium of Saint John's University

The Stadium of the Saint's John's University used to be a poorly-equipped gym. The cornerstone was laid in 1918 but the ceremony for laying the foundation stone was held in 1919.

Location: No. 1575, Wanhangdu Road

圣约翰大学西门堂

（万航渡路 1575 号）

西门堂于 1923 年岁末奠基，次年落成。在沪经商 40 年的美国人西门先生，生前对圣约翰大学的教育事业支持颇多。去世后，其夫人捐资扩建校舍，以纪念亡夫，此即西门堂。1925 年起，西门堂为圣约翰大学附属高中部校舍。

Ximen Hall of Saint John's University

Located in the East China University of Political Science and Law, the hall was completed in 1924. It was once named Dongfeng Building.

Location: No. 1575, Wanhangdu Road

圣约翰大学格致室

(万航渡路 1575 号)

　　格致室的建造资金是由圣约翰大学时任校长卜舫济于清光绪二十三年(1897)赴美募资,加之上海士绅、学生及西方商人的热情捐助而凑得。于光绪二十四年(1898)奠基,光绪二十五年(1899)落成。约大博物院一度设于楼内。1998年华东政法大学扩大招生,此楼改作学生宿舍,并改用原名"格致"为"格致楼"。

Gezhi Chamber of Saint John's University

To build this chamber, F. L. Hawks Pott, then Principal of Saint John's University, went to the US to raise funds in 1897. Overseas students and Western businessmen also donated generously for the construction. Its foundation was laid in 1898; it was completed in 1899.

Location: No. 1575, Wanhangdu Road

民立中学办公楼

（威海路414号）

建于1920年的这幢建筑，由于隶属当年上海的进步学校民立中学而备受世人尊敬。该校为五四运动时期上海学联的发起者之一。

Former Office Building of Minli High School

Constructed in 1920, it was a property of Shanghai Minli High School, which was active in supporting the fight against Japanese invaders.

Location: No. 414, Weihai Road

中国红十字会医院

（乌鲁木齐中路12号）

中国红十字医院于1910年落成，古典主义风格，1962年因医院临近华山路改称华山医院。该建筑现为华山医院办公楼。

Former China Red Cross Hospital

This classical-style building, completed in 1910, now serves as the office building of Huashan Hospital.
Location: No. 12, Middle Urumqi Road

[虹口救火会]

（吴淞路 560 号）

　　此址由当年的工部局投资设计建造，1917 年竣工，是虹口救火会旧址。虹口救火会前身为成立于 1866 年的火政处虹口机队，1915 年迁址于此，改称虹口救火会。

Former Hongkew Fire Station

Designed with some aspects of Renaissance architecture and built by the Shanghai Municipal Council, it was completed in 1917.

Location: No. 560, Wusong Road

大上海大戏院

（西藏中路500号）

该戏院现名大上海电影院，一度改称遵义电影院。建筑由上海融融股份有限公司投资，委托华盖建筑师事务所设计，于1933年建成。该建筑于21世纪初重建，2008年以五星级影院再度开张迎客。

Former Metropol Theatre

Completed in 1933, for some time, it was called the Zunyi Theatre.

Location: No. 500, Middle Tibet Road

大世界游乐场

（西藏南路1号）

　　该建筑始建于1917年，1924年重建。当初是由大商人黄楚九创办经营，开设有游艺杂耍、南北戏曲、曲艺等游乐项目。1930年上海滩青帮头领黄金荣接手经营，该游乐场成为当时中国最大、名闻海内外的综合性游乐场。

Former Great World Amusement Park

Built in 1917, it was remodeled in 1924. In 1930, it was taken over by Huang Jinrong, leader of the Green Gang in Shanghai, and became the largest, most famous multi-functional amusement park in China at the time.

Location: No. 1, South Tibet Road

> 东方饭店

（西藏中路120号）

该饭店建筑于1929年落成，20世纪50年代初这里改作上海市工人文化宫。

The Former Dong Fang Hotel
Completed in 1929, it was transformed into the Shanghai Workers' Cultural Palace in the early 1950s.
Location: No. 120, Middle Tibet Road

| 上海银行同业公会 |

（香港路59号）

　　此建筑1925年建成，上海银行业同业公会1931年于此设立。1933年上海市银行票据交易所于此正式挂牌。1946年起，全市所有中外银行、钱庄之票据交换均在这里办理，从而成为真正意义上的"金融枢纽"。

Former Shanghai Banking Association

Completed in 1925, the Shanghai Banking Association was founded here.

Location: No. 59, Hong Kong Road

延安东路、延安西路、中山东路等
Yan'an Road, West Yan'an Road, East Zhongshan Road, etc.

中汇大厦

（延安东路143号）

中汇大厦原为1929年开业的中汇银行所在地。该银行是由当年上海滩著名大亨杜月笙投资组建。杜月笙出资兴建中汇银行大厦，于1934年落成。当时该大楼内除设有中汇银行外还有各类商行、事务所、办事处、经营部等140余家，属较早的"写字楼"经营模式。1959年，时任上海市市长的陈毅元帅批准将该大楼移交上海博物馆使用。

Former Building of the New Chung Wei Bank

Completed in 1934, it housed the New Chung Wei Bank that opened in 1929.

Location: No. 143, East Yan'an Road

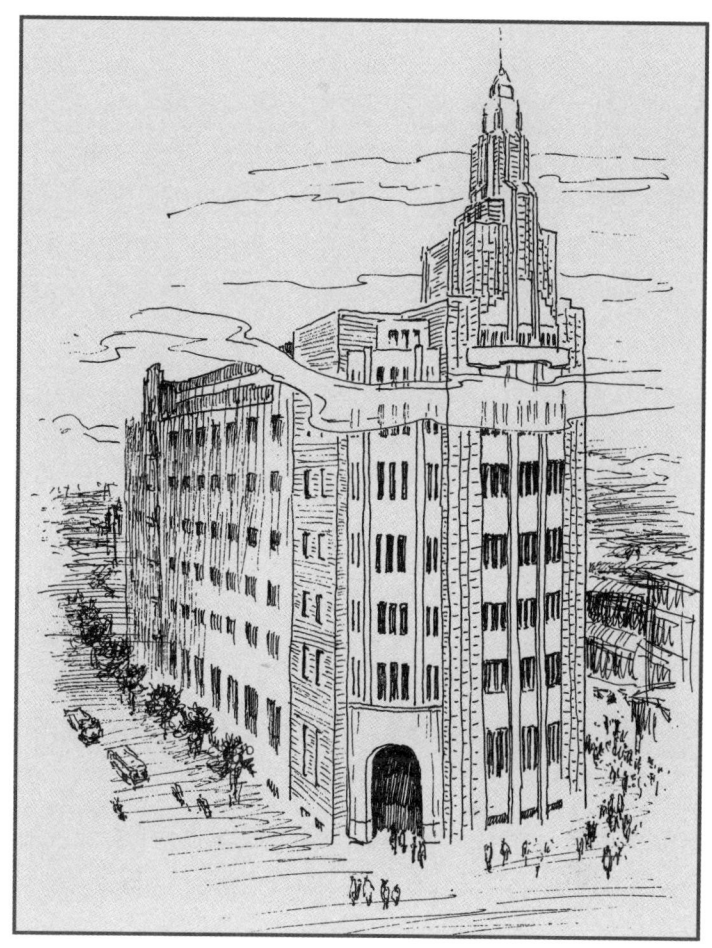

华商纱布交易所

（延安东路260号）

这幢英国古典风格的建筑，建于1923年，是上海的第一座钢筋混凝土建筑，原为华商纱布交易所。1958年上海自然历史博物馆迁入。

Former Shanghai Cotton Goods Exchange

Built in 1923, this classical English building was the first reinforced concrete building in Shanghai. It used to house the Shanghai Cotton Goods Exchange.

Location: No. 260, East Yan'an Road

洋泾浜气象信号台

（延安东路外滩）

　　清光绪十年（1884），法国天主教会在上海创建了徐家汇天文台，同时设立气象信号台。当年的信号台还只是一根高耸的木杆。1907 年，重建圆柱形的气象信号塔，高 36.8 米。1993 年，在外滩改造工程中，信号台被整体向东移位 20 米。

Former Gutzlaff Signal Tower

This meteorological signal tower was built in 1884, when French Jesuits established the Zikawei Observatory.
Location: Bund section, East Yan'an Road

德士古大楼

（延安东路110号）

德士古大楼最早属英商会德丰公司的产业，建于1943年，所以又称会德丰大楼。后来成为了美商德士古石油公司在华总部。

Former Texaco Building
Built in 1943, it was owned by the British Wheelock& Co., thus also called the Wheelock& Co. Building.
Location: No. 110, East Yan'an Road

南京大戏院

（延安东路523号）

20世纪20年代，电影业在上海日益红火。华人名流何挺然的联怡公司在今址西北侧的八仙桥投资建造了南京大戏院。戏院于1930年建成。2003年，因市政建设需要，这座建筑被整体向东南方向平移了66.4米，在内外结构毫发未损的情况下，重新坐落于今天的位置。该戏院如今已改称上海音乐厅。

Former Nanjing Grand Theatre

Funded and designed by Chinese, it has a typical European classic style. The theatre was completed in 1930.
Location: No. 523, East Yan'an Road

宏恩医院

(延安西路221号)

　　这幢建筑是建于1926年的宏恩医院旧址。据悉，这所医院是一位无名氏捐赠给租界工部局的。1950年医院被解放军上海市军管会接管，次年改建为华东医院。

Former Hong'en Hospital
This building was redeveped in 1926 at the site of the former Hong'en Hospital.
Location: No. 221, West Yan'an Road

意大利总会

(延安西路238号)

20世纪初,众多意大利人来上海经商。出于本国侨民交际的需要,他们修建了这幢文艺复兴风格的建筑,开设了意大利总会。建筑于1925年落成。

Former Italian Club

Many Italians came to Shanghai to do business in the early 20th century. They constructed this Renaissance-style building and launched an Italian club for social networking. The building was completed in 1925.

Location: No. 238, West Yan'an Road

美国乡村总会

（延安西路1262号）

美国乡村总会，旧称花旗总会，在上海生物制品研究所内。建于1925～1930年，由邬达克设计。总会原辟有高尔夫球场，保龄球和弹球房、跳舞厅等。

Former Columbia Country Club

Built during 1925-1930, the Columbia Country Club, formerly known as the American Club, has a garden house and an auditorium.
Location: No. 1262, West Yan'an Road

安倍洋行办公楼

（圆明园路97号）

　　这幢楼宇，建于1907年。1936年前的使用情况目前无从查考。1940年瑞士安培洋行设立于此，负责人为蔡文庆和徐子华，主营进口化工原料。

Former Office Building of Swiss Ampire Company
Completed in 1907, it witnessed the founding of the Swiss Ampire Company in 1940.
Location: No. 97, Yuanmingyuan Road

上海自然科学研究所

（岳阳路320号）

20世纪20年代，日本政府用庚子赔款建立了自然科学研究所。这幢自然科学研究所正馆于1930年建成，由日本建筑师设计，带有明显哥特式韵味。

Former Shanghai Institute of Natural Science

The Japanese government established the Shanghai Institute of Natural Science with funds from the Boxer Indemnity, part of one of the Unequal Treaties between China and Japan. This building was finished in 1930.
Location: No. 320, Yueyang Road

第四中山大学医学院

(医学院路138号)

这幢建于1936年的大楼,本属1927年由中国自行创办的第一所国立大学医学院。该学院1932年独立,成为国立上海医学院,系当年全国唯一的国立医学院。

Medical College of the Fourth Zhongshan University
Set up in 1927, it was the first medical school of a national university set up by the Chinese; it was completed in 1936.
Location: No. 138, Medical School Road

杨树浦发电厂

（杨树浦路 2800 号）

工部局 1908 年设立电力处，收购老电厂，并建造了更大规模的电厂，即杨树浦发电厂，1913 年开始供电。

Yangshupu Power Plant

Shanghai Municipal Council established this Electric Power Section. The section acquired old power plants and built the larger Yangshupu Power Plant put into operation in 1913.

Location: No. 2800, Yangshupu Road

杨树浦水厂

(杨树浦路 830 号)

　　始建于清光绪七年(1881),建成于光绪九年(1883)的杨树浦水厂,当时隶属于上海市自来水市北有限公司。该水厂是全国供水行业建厂最早,生产能力最大的地面水厂之一。

Yangshupu Water Plant
Built in 1883, at that time, it was the earliest surface water plant with the largest production capacity in China.
Location: No. 830, Yangshupu Road

怡和纱厂

(杨树浦路670号)

　　怡和纱厂创办于清光绪二十二年(1896)。该纱厂由英商投资,是上海最早的外资工厂,当时以生产"兰龙牌"棉纱享誉盛名。这幢厂房建造于1909~1911年。

Former Jardine Cotton Mill

Established in 1896, it was the earliest foreign-funded factory in Shanghai; this building was constructed between 1909 and 1911.

Location: No. 670, Yangshupu Road

百乐门舞厅

(愚园路218号)

　　这座舞厅由华商顾联承投资,于1932年建成,当时称作"百乐门大饭店舞厅"。建筑风格属近代美国建筑形式。内部配有弹簧地板的大舞池,被誉为"千人舞厅"。

Former Paramount Ballroom

Funded by Chinese businessmen and completed in 1932, it was then called the Paramount Grand Hotel Ballroom.

Location: No. 218, Yuyuan Road

海底电缆登陆局房

（逸仙路3945号）

该建筑始建于清同治十二年（1873），据说当年黄浦江水下电缆常被往来船只的铁锚挂断，后开始架设陆上电缆。

Former Building of the Office for Joining Land and Submarine Cables

It was built in 1873 when land cables were laid because the submarine cables were often broken by anchors in Huangpu River.

Location: No. 3945, Yixian Road

乍浦路桥

（乍浦路越过苏州河处）

　　这座三孔桥梁前身是一座浮桥，由传教士文惠廉集资建造。后于清同治十二年（1873），租界地的工部局将之改建为固定木桥。1927年再次改建成钢筋混凝土结构的现代化桥梁。

Zhapu Road Bridge

The three-arched bridge, formerly a floating bridge, was built with funds raised by the missionary William Jones Boone.
Location: Suzhou Creek, Zhapu Road.

中国通商银行

(中山东路6号)

中国通商银行是华人自办的第一家银行,亦乃中国发行纸币的第一家银行,成立于清光绪二十三年(1897),由清末官商,洋务派代表人物,被誉为"中国实业之父"和"中国商父"的盛宣怀创办。这幢建筑便是该行总行所在地,于1906年建造。

Former Commercial Bank of China

The bank wasestablished by Sheng Hsuan-Huai, a famous businessman of the late Qing Dynasty (1840-1911).Built in 1906, it was the first bank set up by the Chinese. This building housed its headquarters.
Location: No. 6, East Zhongshan Road

亚细亚火油公司大楼

（中山东一路1号）

亚细亚火油公司大楼，是一座折中主义风格的建筑。1899年，麦克倍恩公司买下了这里的房地产，并于1913年拆旧建新，1916年建成了这座当时的"外滩第一楼"。

The Former British and Royal Dutch Shell's Asiatic Petroleum Division
Bought by McBain Company, it was built into the then "First Building on the Bund" in 1916.
Location: No. 1, East Zhongshan Road Number One

英国总会

（中山东一路2号）

　　1861年在沪英国侨民发起创办英国总会，又名上海总会。1864年建楼，1909年拆旧建新，1910年这幢新楼落成并启用。这里乃当时重要的社交场所之一。

Former British Club

The former Shanghai Club, also named as British Club, was founded by the English Natimals in Shanghai in Shanghai in 1861.

Location: No. 2, East Zhongshan Road Number One

有利银行

（中山东一路4号）

　　这幢建筑原名联合大楼，因其为美国有利银行所有，故亦称有利银行大楼。其于1916年建成，属仿文艺复兴建筑风格。

Former Building of Mercantile Bank of India, London, and China

Built in 1916 and originally named the Union Building, it was renamed the American Mercantile Bank of India, London and China Building as it was owned by the bank.

Location: No. 4, East Zhongshan Road Number One

大北电报公司

(中山东一路7号)

　　该建筑竣工于1907年。这是幢假五层的原大北电报公司大楼，系法国文艺复兴风格。

Former Great Northern Telegraph Corporation
Former Great Northern Telegraph Corporation Building finished in 1907, it is typical French Renaissance style.
Location: No. 7, East Zhongshan Road Number One

上海轮船招商局

（中山东一路9号）

这里原是旗昌洋行的花园，19世纪70年代转让给轮船招商局。1901年招商局在靠外滩一侧的花园上建造了这幢三层办公楼。

China Merchants Steamship Navigation Company

Originally as the garden of Russell & Co, it was later taken over by the China Merchants Steamship Navigation Company which started by Li Hongzhang, a famous minister in late Qing Dynasty. China Merchants Group constructed this three-story office building on the site of the garden on the Bund in 1901.

Location: No. 9, East Zhongshan Road Number One

汇丰银行

（中山东一路 10～12 号）

　　这座大楼建于 1923 年，属上海近代建筑史中的极品之一。汇丰银行上海分行早在 1874 年就在这里建造营业场所，1921 年拆旧建新，竣工时曾被英国人誉为"从苏伊士运河到白岭海峡的一座最讲究的建筑"。

Former HSBC Building
Constructed in 1923, it has a neo-classical dome, best representing Shanghai's modern architecture.
Location: No. 10 to 12, East Zhongshan Road Number One

| 华俄道胜银行 |

(中山东一路15号)

　　这幢建成于1902年的豪华建筑是上海第一幢采用瓷砖贴面的楼宇,且系最早安装卫生设备和电梯的建筑之一。

Former Building of the Russo-Chinese Bank
Completed in 1902, this luxurious building was the earliest with tile facing, sanitary facilities and elevators in Shanghai.
Location: No. 15, East Zhongshan Road Number One

上海海关大楼

(中山东一路13号)

这座海关大楼落成于1927年,是20世纪20年代上海外滩最高的建筑物。

Shanghai Customs House

Completed in 1927, this was the tallest building on the Bund in the 1920s.

Location: No. 13, East Zhongshan Road Number One

交通银行

（中山东一路14号）

该建筑地块最初是英国著名宝顺洋行的产业，19世纪下半叶被德国德华银行买下，并建造了一座文艺复兴风格的大楼。1928年交行总部迁至这里。

Former Building of China Bank of Communications

Constructed by the Deutsch-Asiatische Bank, it was later taken over by the Shanghai Branch of the China Bank of Communications. The Bank has headquartered here since 1928.

Location: No. 14, East Zhongshan Road Number One

> 台湾银行

（中山东一路16号）

这座建筑兴建于1924年，为设立于1911年的日商台湾银行上海分行办公大楼。

Former Building of the Japanese Bank of Taiwan
Completed in 1924, to house the Japanese Bank of Taiwan.
Location: No. 16, East Zhongshan Road Number One

《字林西报》报馆

（中山东一路17号）

《字林西报》为当时著名的英文报纸，前身为《北华捷报》。这座报社大楼由英国德和洋行于1924年建造。

Building of *Former North China Daily News*

North China Daily News was a famous English-language newspaper then, formally known as North China Herald. The building was built by Leste, Johnson Morris (the UK) in 1924.

Location: No. 17, East Zhongshan Road Number One

麦加利银行

（中山东一路18号）

  这座建筑是原麦加利银行大楼，建成于1923年。1955年，改为春江大楼。

Former Chartered Bank of India, Australia, and China

Completed in 1923, the Greek Renaissance classical style building, houses the Chartered Bank of India Australia and China.

Location: No. 18, East Zhongshan Road Number One

中国银行大楼

（中山东一路23号）

此地原是上海德国总会，后由中国银行购得，于1922年改建成银行营业楼。1934年建造新楼，1937年建成。

Bank of China Building

Built on the site of the old German Club, it was purchased by the Bank of China as an operational center.

Location: No. 23, East Zhongshan Road Number One

> 沙逊大厦

(中山东一路20号)

此大厦由英资新沙逊洋行下属的华懋地产股份有限公司投资建造。1929年新楼落成。今为和平饭店北楼。

The Former Sassoon House
It served as the office building for the Shanghai Branch of the New Sassoon Bank. In 1956, it was converted into the "Peace Hotel". Now, it's the North Building of the hotel.
Location: No. 20, East Zhongshan Road Number One

正金银行

(中山东一路24号)

建于1924年的该建筑原为老沙逊洋行的产业,后被日本横滨的正金银行购得。新中国成立后,这里由上海市纺织管理局使用,故又叫"纺织大楼"。

Former Yokohama Specie Bank

Completed in 1924, after the PRC was founded, the building became the headquarters of the Shanghai Textile Industry Bureau; thus it was also called the "Textile Building".

Location: No. 24, East Zhongshan Road Number One

扬子大楼

（中山东一路 26 号）

扬子大楼原属扬子水火保险公司所有，1922年落成。而后大楼被保宁、中华等多家保险公司租用，故一度被称为"保险大楼"。

Yangtze Insurance Building

Completed in 1922, it was owned by the Yangtze Insurance Association Ltd.

Location: No. 26, East Zhongshan Road Number One

东方汇理银行上海分行

(中山东一路29号甲)

新中国成立后改名为"东方大楼",1914年建成并投入使用。此建筑是外滩迄今仅剩的一幢三层楼房,是外滩建筑群中仅有的法国人出资建造之作。

Former Shanghai Branch of the French Banque de l'Indochine

It is the only three-storey building remaining on the Bund. It was renamed "Oriental Building", after the People's Republic of China (PRC) was founded.

Location: Building A, No. 29, East Zhongshan Road Number One

怡和洋行办公楼

(中山东一路 27 号)

这幢建筑竣工于 1922 年，曾为英商怡和洋行办公楼。1955 年收归国有后，长期由上海市外贸局使用，因而也被人们称作"外贸大楼"。

Former British Jardine Matheson Building
Completed in 1922, to house the then powerful Jardine Matheson Company.
Location: No. 27, East Zhongshan Road Number One

英国总领事馆

(中山东一路33号)

原英国总领事馆位于黄浦江边，由英国设计师设计，清同治十二年（1873）竣工。该建筑为典型的外廊式建筑，砖木结构，英国文艺复兴风格。

The Former Consulate General of the United Kingdom

Built in 1873 at the Huangpu River, it was a masterpiece of two British designers. The building is typical English Renaissance style.

Location: No. 33, East Zhongshan Road Number One

十六铺码头

（中山东二路531号）

19世纪中叶，十六铺地区用于驳船、洋船卸货登岸的木质漂浮码头出现，不久又改进为木质固定码头。20世纪初，供轮船专用的钢质浮码头、固定码头相继建成。

16-Shop Wharf

In the mid-19th century, this was an area where floating wooden wharf were used for unloading cargo from barges and ocean ships; the floating wharf were later replaced by fixed ones also made of wood.

Location: No. 531, East Zhongshan Road Number Two

| 上海电话局南市总局 |

（中华路734号）

　　1920年，交通部购得此建筑地块，并动工兴建上海电话局大厦，次年大厦落成。

Former Nanshi Branch of Shanghai Telephone Office

The Ministry of Communications acquired this building block in 1920 and built it into the Shanghai Telephone Station Building, completed in 1921.

Location: No. 734, Zhonghua Road

其他
Others

白鹤塘湾桥

（青浦区白鹤镇）

白鹤塘湾桥初名庆泽桥，建于明万历二十三年（1595），清乾隆五十四年（1789）重建。清咸丰三年（1853），上海爆发小刀会起义，塘湾村农民起义领袖周立春、周秀英曾在该桥上杀退清兵。

Tangwan Bridge

Originally named Qingze Bridge, it is located in Tangwan Village, Baihe Town, Qingpu District, Shanghai. Built in 1595 and renovated in 1849, it crosses the Aiqi River.

Location: Baihe Town, Qingpu District

放生桥

（青浦区朱家角镇）

放生桥建于明隆庆五年（1571），横跨于镇东首漕港河上。五孔石拱，是上海地区最长、最大、最高的五孔石拱桥，称为"沪上第一桥"。

Fangsheng Bridge

Fangsheng ("Free captive animals") Bridge was built in 1571, as a five-arched stone bridge.
Location: Zhujiajiao Town, Qingpu District

望仙桥

（松江区方塔园）

望仙桥，具体建造年代不详，但至少是建于南宋嘉熙年间（1237～1240）之前，属单跨平板石桥。桥面本亦有木栏，今已无存。

Wangxian Bridge

The bridge is located in the southeast corner of Fangta Garden, Songjiang District. It is believed to have been built before the Southern Song Dynasty Jiaxi reign period (1237-1240). It is a single-span stone beam.

Location: Fangtayuan, Songjiang District

济渡桥

(金山区漕泾镇水库村)

济渡桥亦称七星桥,俗名刘家渡桥。建于清同治十三年(1874),落成于清光绪三年(1877)。

Jidu Bridge
Also called Seven Stars Bridge, it was completed in 1877.
Location: Shuiku Village, Caojing Town, Jinshan District

古漪园

（嘉定西南翔镇沪宜路 218 号）

该园当初是明万历年间（1573～1620）河南通判闵士籍之私家花园，原称奇园。清乾隆十一年（1746），洞庭山人叶锦购得后改名古漪园。

Guyi Garden
The garden was owned by magistrate Min Shiji during the Ming Wanli reign period (1573-1620). It was previously named Qi Garden.
Location: No. 218, Huyi Road, Nan Xiang Town, Jiading District

学宫牌坊

（崇明城桥镇鳌山路696号）

崇明学宫始建于元泰定四年（1327），明天启二年（1622）重修。学宫内现有除东西牌坊外，还有棂星门、泮池等诸多明清建筑群。

Memorial Archway Gates, Chongming Academy

Built in 1327 and restored in 1622, it includes Ming Dynasty (1368-1644) and Qing Dynasty (1644-1911) structures such as the memorial archway gates and the Pan Pond (a pool in front of the academy).

Location: No. 696, Aoshan Road, Chengqiao Town, Chongming County

州桥

（嘉定区州桥风貌区）

此桥建于南宋开禧年间（1205～1207）。这里是嘉定城镇的发祥地。南宋嘉定十一年（1218）嘉定建县即设于此。

Zhouqiao Bridge

It is located in Zhouqiao an area of historical and cultural significance in Shanghai. Jiading District was developed in this area. The bridge was built between 1205 and 1207 during Southern Song Dynasty (1127 - 1279).

Location: Zhouqiao, Jiading District.

[报童]

　　上海街头的报童主要盛行于民国时期。而有关上海报童最为人们所熟知的事情，则莫过于著名音乐家聂耳所作的《卖报歌》了。

Paperboy
The number of paperboys reached its highest point during the Republic of China Period 1912-1949.

修伞匠

据悉，我国用伞的历史已有数千年。宋朝以后，即已出现皮纸伞、油纸伞、布伞等。民国时期，江南的手工业十分发达，绸布花伞亦是上海市民所爱。此外，由于西方商贸在上海的兴盛，洋伞在这里也十分流行。为此，修伞匠在上海是不可或缺的。

Umbrella Repairer

During the Republic of China Period (1912-1949), the handicraft industry thrived in regions south of the Yangtze River. Umbrellas made of figured silk were popular in Shanghai, thus making the umbrella repairer indispensable.

弹花匠

弹棉花这一行业起源于海南崖州黎族部落。在上海，做新棉被或翻新棉被叫弹棉花；从事这门手艺的人叫弹花匠。

Cotton-Fluffing Bedding

Cotton-fluffing for making bedding was popular from the 19th century to the 1950s-1960s.

剃头匠

民国时期，理发店还不太盛行，剃头业大多还是以露天摆摊为主。在上海从事这一行当者多来自扬州。

Barber

During the Republic of China Period (1912-1949), barbershops were not common. Barbers then mainly set up stalls along the streets.

沪上印度人

第二次世界大战后到上海来的印度人，大多从事保安类的服务性行业。

Indians in Shanghai

Indians who came to Shanghai after World War II, mostly worked in the field of security service.

修铜匠

　　20世纪前半叶，江南民间使用铜器还很普遍。因而对使用破损的铜器予以修理，便成为一种市场需求。不过铜制品修补是一个有着相当技术含量的行当，其中有煅烧、锤打、打磨、酸洗等十余道工序。

Coppersmith

In the first half of the 20th century, copper wares were commonly used in regions south of the Yangtze River, thus there was a good market for worn copper ware repair.